Working
from a
Home Office
Successfully

Working from a Home Office Successfully

Best Practice Tips

Cecelia Jernegan

Outskirts Press, Inc.
Denver, Colorado

Working from a Home Office Successfully
Best Practice Tips

Outskirts Press, Inc.
http://www.outskirtspress.com

ISBN: 978-1-4327-5145-6

Outskirts Press and the "OP" logo are trademarks belonging to Outskirts Press, Inc.

This book is dedicated to my husband, two sons, and grandchildren, plus countless family and friends who have encouraged me to be me. To my dad, mom, and sister who are no longer in this physical world but with me every day in my heart.

I also wish to thank the hundreds of hardworking employees who work from a home office environment or from a regular office. Your tips, best practices, and advice will definitely make an impact on others as well.

This book is a short guideline to help those who read it find in today's world a "healthy and happy" work/life balance working from a home office environment.

Contents

Learn from me – Been there.........done that!

I have always wondered how an OB/GYN that never had a baby could explain what labor pains truly "feel like." It just seems to me that if you've been through a certain event, it is much easier to educate, coach, and teach someone else what to expect.

That is why I have written this book on working from a home office environment. Not only have I tried and failed several times myself, but I have become successful and currently coach others with the best practice tips. I've learned from many others much wiser than me. I have trained and coached many to work from a home office. I have seen many people become very successful and many others fail miserably.

Here is the secret. There is no one secret. There is no magic bullet.

However, there are best practices to be followed and learned. Just like exercising a muscle every day, if a "routine" is adopted, YOU will be successful too. The true secret is consistency and discipline combined with a few other tips. This secret sounds easy, but don't be fooled.

People who work from home must have an "entrepreneurship spirit." That basically means they have the _desire_ to be successful working for themselves. No one needs to light the fire under their feet. The fire to be successful burns within them!

I have been fortunate over the years to be employed by major companies and also operate and own my own businesses.

Owning your own business is self-rewarding. You do not have to answer to anyone else but yourself. However, when owning a business of any type, you work 24 hours, 7 days a week. You might not be physically working, but the business is always in your head. You can't escape!

That is the same concept when working from a home office. You could work 24/7 if you chose to do so.

Balancing work/home becomes an interesting tightrope. The lines between the two can become blurred.

However, in today's world it is easier than ever

to work from home given all the new and ever-changing technology.

My first experience working from home was over 10 years ago. Now you must remember, technology continues to improve daily. When I first started in a home office, BlackBerries and laptops were barely on the scene. Working from home meant you were chained to you home phone and your oversized computer. Today's world is quite different. Technology now affords us the luxury of working from a home office to mean "anywhere" and at "any time." I have been physically in one location returning e-mails and conducting 3 conference calls in a 2-hour time span. That location was NOT my home office. In today's world, you can take your office wherever you go. As long as you have the right technology, you can work and play almost simultaneously. You must be able to multitask effectively.

My first home office was a total failure. I organized my desk, phone, printer, and computer in the living room close to the TV.

Now you must have a mental picture of how effective I was going to be with that setup.

My employer at that time expected me to call clients over the phone, visit clients on occasion, and sell, sell, sell their product.

Deep down I am a salesperson. I have been told by many I could sell snow to an Eskimo. I guess

I could. And if the Eskimo did not like white snow, I would invent a way to make red, blue, green, and orange snow. My mind is basically one of a salesperson. Putting a salesperson in a home office with very little social interaction became an issue for me, something I had not been prepared to deal with at the time.

I believe all of us have a little "salesperson" mentality. We enjoy interacting with others. However, working out of the home office day in and day out does NOT afford the luxury to meet and interact with others.

The one situation working in a home office environment that is underscored is that daily "social interaction" is limited. There have been numerous studies conducted about office interaction, the pro's and con's. If you are one that has been in an office environment, be warned that you will find a home office difficult to adapt to the first few months. You will be going to the grocery stores looking for someone to interact and communicate with on a personal level.

My first home office was set up in the living room close to the TV. I can tell you from experience you need a separate room, preferably with a door. Trust me on this one. I have visited many other home offices over the past 8 years. The very best and most successful understand about the "location" of their office in their home. We will talk more about office setup in the next chapter.

I originally was not prepared for all the distractions I would encounter in my first home office environment. I thought it was great I could stay on top of company work and my "honey do's" lists that needed to be accomplished around my home. For example: emptying the dishwasher, sweeping the floor, picking weeds in the backyard, grocery shopping, paying the bills, cleaning the swimming pool, picking up the kids from school, dusting, washing the clothes, mowing the grass, etc. Now remember: if you are working from a home office, you should be on a schedule with at least an 8- to 10-hour shift with time off for lunch.

These "home chores" I just mentioned will cut into your 8-hour shift. Get my point? It is easy at the end of the week to have a clean house and an impeccable yard but no sales calls or appointments scheduled for the following week.

It is not easy to balance your home life and your home office if you do not have discipline. You MUST adhere to a daily routine and schedule. It is so simple to be thrown off course due to one major issue. For example, one time I was working from my home office and the cable in my neighborhood went down.

Carpenters were building a new home down the street and cut into the cable line. Now remember I told you I failed miserably with my first home office.

That is how we learn by failing. Hopefully with my examples, you will remember them as you set up and work out of your own home office. With the cable being down, I thought that gave me a free ticket for the day. I was not disciplined enough to continue my work without the Internet. I ended up spending most of the day working in the yard. It was a beautiful sunny day and the roses needed pruning and the garden needed irrigating. Of course later in the afternoon around 4:00 pm, the cable was back on. By then it was time to shut down my home office. What a sad excuse for a wasted workday. Nothing was accomplished. I said I would help you to understand the Do's and the <u>Don'ts</u>! This day was a definite "don't" day.

I could have gone out on that day making sales calls, or I could have done extensive telemarketing on the phone. But I used the cable "going out" as an excuse not to work. And who would know? Of course at the end of the month, my sales quota could have been compromised.

To be successful in a home office, each day must count. Each day is a day to excel and achieve. One lost workday cannot be made up at the end of the month.

Someone much wiser than me who worked from a home office told me each day she woke, she dressed and put on her makeup before she started her workday. I thought the whole idea of working from home was so you could wear your pajamas all day long. This comment made to me was from a very smart businesswoman. I believe it to be true. It is hard to be professional over the phone when you look and feel like a bum. Get my point here? Now I am not saying you need to dress like you are going to the prom. If you feel professional, you will perform professionally.

Every day it is important to be consistent. When you begin your workday, perform the same routine every single workday. It is very easy in a home office to have your routine interrupted. I had neighbors stop by because they lost their cat and needed my assistance. Or their car broke down 5 miles outside of town. Your friends, family, and neighbors know you work from home. They think you are sitting there doing nothing!

You must make them understand you are running and operating YOUR business. You are working. Just like you are working in an office environment, you cannot drop everything to fix a "pop up" situation or problem. You must guard your time. You should have a pretty good idea by now about the do's and don'ts. I highly recommend you read Steven Covey's book *The 7 Habits of Highly Effective People*. It is worth every penny spent!

Chapter 1 Best Practices: ━━━━━━━━━━

1. Adhere to a routine.
2. Dress for success.
3. Manage your time and be consistent with your routine each day.
4. Let others know you are working and guard your time.
5. Don't let the "home chores" interrupt your workday – stay focused and disciplined.

Office Setup

Setting up your office is critical, as the wrong room or the wrong environment could cause you to fail. As I mentioned in Chapter 1, my first home office was a disaster. I organized my office in the living room close to the TV.

I have found the best home offices are in a separate room with a door that closes for privacy.

I have seen many home offices set up in the guest bedroom. They take the time to set up the computer, fax/copy machine, desk, etc. They normally have everything perfect and a door that closes. Then once or twice a month, they have "guests" that come to visit. Guess what happens? You do not have access to your office. Or you need your guests to get up early and leave the "guest bedroom" because you have to go to work. You need to think what will be the best room for your home office. Now, obviously if you only have in-laws visit over the Christmas holiday, then you should be fine. But if you have aunts, uncles, cousins, mothers, or dads that are regular visitors, then I would rule out the guest bedroom for your home office.

I have also seen colleagues who are working out of the home office use their kitchen table for their office. I can tell you that in most homes, the kitchen is a very busy place. Perhaps if you are a bachelor and you eat out every night, then the kitchen table may be a logical place for your home office.

In reality, find a place in your home that is secluded, has a door, and is a place where you do not have to constantly be moving your computer and equipment.

As far as the office setup, I have seen some remarkable home offices. I have seen people that have spent thousands of dollars on desks, chairs, filing cabinets, bookshelves, etc. I have always thought the person who thinks and acts like a CEO will probably end up being a CEO. If you act like you are a poor starving college student and your laptop is sitting on a cardboard box, then that frame of mind will stay with you as you work.

I recommend you find a happy medium. It is crucial you have an ergonomically correct desk and chair. If you are going to spend hours sitting at your desk and typing on your computer, you'd better have good positioning for your neck, back, and spine. If not, years from now you will have a crooked neck with arthritis and tendonitis giving you much pain for years to come. And watch your eyes. Make sure you have proper lighting. Be smart about what type of equipment you purchase for your new home office. Also, when you purchase a copy or fax or copy/fax machine, there will be no one to help you when the machine breaks down. Most people in a home office most likely will be all by themselves. Make sure you understand how the equipment you purchased works. That way if the equipment does malfunction, you can easily fix it yourself. Also, the telephone is crucial. Your cell phone reception is just as important as well. I would recommend you have both a cell phone and a landline phone. The reason is that cell phones could potentially cause brain cancer. Now is this fact or fiction? Do you want to be the one to test on your brain whether this is fact or fiction?

Then use your cell phone for the quick office calls. But when you have conference calls or telephone calls that are going to take over 10 minutes, having a landline is advantageous. The great thing is that in today's world, if you leave your home office, you can transfer the number to ring on your cell phone.

With your home phone, it is important you have the best plan available. Do your research in your city or market to find out the best provider. The telephone provider should have unlimited long distance, especially if you are going to be calling out of state. Be careful if you have international calls and make sure again you have the best provider for your landline phone depending on your needs. That is the same for your cell phone. Look for the best plan that will suit your needs. You may have to change your plan as your business grows. Make sure you monitor your monthly calls until you have a good idea that you have the best plan for both the landline phone and the cell phone.

Your home office Internet provider is probably more important than you phone provider – the reason being that you must have confidence your provider not only has excellent consistent service, but what happens when the service is disrupted? Does the provider have a help desk or 800# you can call 24/7? Remember, if you wake up at 2:00 am in the morning and you want to work, your provider needs to be providing you service and dependability.

When searching for a provider in your area, conduct your research on their company. Contact others that have been using their service. Ask for testimonials from their customers.

It goes without saying that your office should be organized just as if you are working in a regular office. Take time to decorate your office with motivational pictures, family pictures, and special plaques so the office reflects you.

Each day when you walk into your home office, you should feel motivated with your surroundings. You should want to sit at your desk, and when you look around smile at what you have created.

Never leave your desk or work area at the end of the day a mess. It is hard to begin a new workday when you have to start by cleaning up from the day before.

Another great idea is to purchase all your supplies and have plenty on hand. There is no reason why during a conference call you should be running around the house looking for a pencil or pen. And keep the supplies organized in your desk drawers. Have pens, pencils, pencil sharpeners, scissors, tape, paper clips, copy paper, folders, and printer ink in a specific place. Keep a running list of supplies that need to be purchased. That way you won't be running out of supplies during the middle of the work week.

Chapter 2 Best Practices: ━━━━━━━━━

1. Situate your home office in a room prefer-ably with a door that closes.
2. Keep the home office out of high traffic areas.
3. Purchase equipment that ergonomically makes sense for your office.
4. Conduct due diligence on your phone, cell phone, and Internet providers.
5. Set your office up as a reflection of you.
6. Buy office supplies and store them in your office, not dispersed throughout the rest of the house.

CHAPTER 3

Discipline

Discipline and consistency go hand in hand. When working in a home office, discipline needs to be your friend. You must understand that you are in charge and responsible for you.

The quote "your self-worth is directly tied into your own consistent habits" has a lot of merit. Think about it. Consistent good habits are key to success.

Your productivity working from a home office is directly related to your daily habits. If you sleep in, spend 2 hours at lunchtime, too much time talking on the phone to family and friends or playing on the computer, then at the end of the month you will have not reached any goals.

It is imperative you have goals for yourself. Perhaps you have a boss or supervisor you report to and the goals will be set for you.

Break your goals down for the month and analyze what tasks need to be accomplished each day to reach those goals.

For example, if you need to conduct 100 sales calls in 1 month and you have a 5-day work week, you will need to complete 25 calls per week, or 5 calls per day. Those 5 calls per day will be a goal you will have to discipline yourself to achieve every day.

If, for some reason, you are only going to work 4 days in a week, then you will need to make 10 calls in 1 day for that particular 4-day work week. If you are an entrepreneur and have no supervisor, then you will have to set your own goals. What do you want to achieve? Break your goals down by month, then by day. That will give you an idea of what needs to be achieved by you each and every day. The secret is that you have to have the discipline and be consistent each and every single day. If you have a day that has an unexpected event (which in today's world is the norm: ex: kids are sick, husband wrecks the car, computer blows up, printer breaks down – you get the picture, right?), you have to be disciplined enough to know you are not going to make your goals unless you make up for the missed work.

That is the essence of discipline. Knowing how to reach your goals and not making excuses. Let's use dieting as an example. Say you know you want to lose 25 pounds. That is your goal. In order to lose the weight, you must increase your level of activity and decrease your calories. You must be very disciplined with your approach.

With all the weight loss books that have been written, it is really pretty simple. Increase one's activities and decrease the calories. Or as others have said, "move more, eat less." However, the roadblock to reaching your goal of losing 25 pounds is how "disciplined" you can be. If you have ever tried to lose weight, quit smoking, stop excessive drinking, or quit any other bad habit, discipline is the key. It is mind over matter, right? Really, the question you need to ask yourself is "Why?" It is all about the "why" for you. It is the same theory and philosophy when working from a home office. Why do you need to have discipline each and every day? The "why" is because you want to succeed.

The reason why is to accomplish your goals. If you don't have goals for yourself, then it is like driving from Los Angeles to New York. You think you know the way, but having a road map (or goals) will make getting to your end destination faster and probably more economical too.

Having goals for yourself is a road map for how to go from point A to point B. But just like losing weight, there are all kinds of obstacles to prevent you from being successful working from your home office. When you first start working from your home office, you will have to start building up the discipline. It is not something you will acquire the first day you walk into your new home office.

It will be very exciting to buy the furniture, decorate your office, and set up the office. But once the office is set up, then the real work begins. Achieving discipline takes a conscious effort each day.

Just like dieting, there are steps you need to take to be successful. For example, when dieting it is best to write down everything you are eating. That way you are very conscious of the amount of food you are consuming. In order to lose 25 pounds (your goal), you need to take direct and targeted action steps and be consistent.

It is the same theory when working in your home office, as it is extremely important to have a daily routine. I will give you an example of a successful routine:

5:00 am
Wake up

5:15 am to 6:15 am
Review e-mails delivered the night before. Read stories and article of interest on the Internet.

6:15 am – 6:30 am
Prepare for physical exercise, get the kids ready for school, officially start your day.

6:30 am – 7:30 am
Physical exercise: walk, run, go to the gym. Your body and mind must both be healthy.

7:30 am – 8:00 am
Shower and dress for the day
Eat breakfast (not at your desk!)

8:00 am – 12:30 pm
Uninterrupted work

12:30 pm – 1:00 pm
Lunch and walk (get out of your office)

1:00pm – 3:00 pm
Uninterrupted work

3:00pm – 3:15pm
Leave the office and stretch neck and back.

3:15 pm – 4:30 pm
Uninterrupted work

4:30 pm – 5:30 pm
Clean up desk; set up appointments and calendar for following day.

This schedule seems pretty simple, right? It takes

discipline to be consistent with your schedule each and every day.

Just like dieting to lose the weight, your discipline will be tempted. You will have interruptions and unexpected events. However, like losing weight, you must keep the goal in mind.

If you are going to be successful working out of a home office, then you must exercise the muscle of discipline. And like building up a muscle, you will need to work on the aspects of discipline each and every day. Discipline will assist you to reach your goals. At first it is not going to be easy.

You will find that the longer you work from your home office, you will find the right schedule that will work for you.

The beauty of working from home is you can design your schedule within a 24-hour time frame. Your schedule does not have to be 8:00 am to 5:00 pm. You can work from 4:00 am to noon if that works for you. Or you can work a split shift from 7:00 am to 11:00 am and 6:00 pm to 10 pm. The key is to reach and accomplish your goals and be able to also have a true and rich work/life balance.

Easier said than done, but it can be accomplished. The secret in one word is "discipline."

Chapter 3 Best Practices ━━━━━━━

1. Daily Discipline Goals
2. Daily Consistency
3. Set realistic goals — know what you need to accomplish in order to reach your daily, monthly, and yearly goals.
4. Have a routine and adhere to it.
5. Be prepared for interruptions and unexpected events.

CHAPTER **4**

Motivation

How will you stay motivated day in and day out? I remember interviewing with the president of a large company when he asked me this exact question. I thought at the time and knew my answer right away: "I would have to motivate myself!" In the 21st century with the Internet, there are countless motivational Web sites. My favorite is "Simple Truths" by Mac Mcpherson. I have an e-mail sent to my "in-box" each morning from his Web site.

I always start the day with reading one of his uplifting thoughts. I also enjoy enriching others and many times forward these motivational thoughts. What a way to start a day, motivating yourself and sharing inspirations with those you care and love. I call this "yoga for your mind." Each day, read an inspiration or watch a short video before you start your day. Take the time to motivate yourself. You are in charge of your own attitude each and every day.

This exercise for the mind takes less than 3 minutes. I also enjoy Zig Ziglar's e-mail messages. Zig has uplifting thoughts that can be sent to your inbox as well. This exercise takes all of 2 minutes to read, ponder, and move on. Now don't get carried away and spend half the morning trying to motivate yourself. A 5-minute shot of inspiration is all you should need.

When my children were young we always called each day of the week by these names:

- Marvelous Monday
- Terrific Tuesday
- Wonderful Wednesday
- Thrilling Thursday
- Fantastic Friday

Sometimes before I shut the computer off in the evening, I would e-mail myself with one of these sayings above in the subject line. When I start my next workday, the subject line always makes me remember the new day is something to celebrate.

Different people are motivated by different thoughts. The one inspiration I have learned is

"Attitude definitely determines your Altitude."

It is up to you and only you how you will begin your day.

There are a ton of negative influences in today's world. I have been running through the airports in major cities and have noticed thousands of people glued to CNN. I have also had the *USA Today* newspaper slipped under my door when I stayed at hotels across America. Of course, this newspaper, as with other papers at hotels and resorts, is a "complimentary" amenity. What a depressing way to start your day. The news seems to focus on the negative. Of course, it is important to stay on top of global and local news.

You must insulate your mind from the negativity. Choose what you want to read and how much of the information you want to accept. If I go to a movie and the ending is very negative, I change the ending to be a happy ending. Or I might even ask if the movie has a great uplifting ending. If it does not, then I will not pay good money for a downer to my brain. There are a ton of Web sites and even people (professional life coaches) who have degrees that teach courses on positive psychology. The book *The Secret* is basically about the law of attraction. If you believe it and think it, then it can happen. However, believing and thinking without "real action" is only a daydream.

You can wish to be healthy. Without reducing

intake of bad calories and increasing activity, your thoughts of being well and healthy will only be a daydream. Taking responsibility for your actions and responsibility for your attitude is only up to one person, and that is you. When working in a home office, there will always be personal issues to deal with. A death of a family member, a divorce, the loss of your home, the loss of a job, a car wreck, a flat tire, just everyday living. Professionally you may find your organization downsizing, layoffs, and reorganizing. Your region or territory may change; you may be assigned to move overseas or move to China.

Whatever happens in an office environment, there are others to reach out to and share these personal or professional issues. When you are working in a home environment, you are left on your own to deal with everyday circumstances. It is important to have a local networking organization.

It is important to have family, friends and co-workers to reach out to. That is the next chapter on "Relationships and Networking."

Best Practices Chapter 4 ━━━━━━━━━

1. Start your day with positive mind stimulations.
2. E-mail yourself messages to your in-box with positive messages the night before.
3. Simple Truths & Zig Ziglar are highly recommended Web sites.
4. Monitor the amount of news and negative thoughts that perpetrate your world.
5. Reach out to others for reinforcement.

Networking/Relationships/Social Interaction

Social interaction was for me the biggest challenge when I first started working from a home office ("virtual office" as some may call it). I am very much a people person.

I thrive on having people around me to communicate and bounce ideas off of them. My first 90 days, I felt so totally alone and isolated. I had very little communication from my corporate office. I would go for weeks and no one seemed to care if I was in my office or not. I remember thinking I could be out suntanning around my swimming pool and no one would know or really care.

The good thing is my #1 strength is responsibility. It would have gone against my total being to be sitting around doing nothing. I cared and wanted to make a difference. I worked and worked hard. Then I figured out that in order to be noticed by my organization, I would have to work twice as hard to receive half of the recognition and praise. Because I was in a virtual office and no one could see, hear, or know what I was accomplishing, I had to "toot my own horn."

I could never move up in the organization because no one knew what I was doing. That is where working in a home office environment sets employees up to be very vulnerable.

It is important you document your day. You must give feedback to your supervisors what production is going on. Now if you are in sales, your numbers at the end of the month will speak for themselves. If you are writing a novel for a publishing company, you will have a deadline to meet. If you are working for yourself, then the amount of money you make at the end of the year will allow you to know if you are being successful or not working from home.

Being totally alone day in and day out can take a toll. It is very important to find other sources of networking. There are several organizations that meet weekly, monthly, or quarterly. I would highly recommend you join a weekly organization. That way you will have social interaction and not go for weeks or months without seeing actual people.

In today's high-tech world, a home office employee can go for weeks and not even see another human being. We are social animals and have a need for human contact.

Networking and relationships go hand in hand. I have learned it is not what you know but who you know. That is what the networking is all about. Networking is all about knowing someone who knows someone else to help you achieve a goal or an objective. If you are really lucky and you are networking with someone you really admire and care about, that can turn into a wonderful relationship. Great relationships, whether they are family, friends, or colleagues, are important for you during times of happiness. You will need these relationships even more during times of stress or hardship that at times are outside of your area of control.

Social interaction, networking, and relationship building, just like motivating yourself, takes time, practice, and constant awareness. Working in a home office limits our ability.

However, with the Internet, the whole world is available at our fingertips. Fifty years ago, people networked, socialized, and built relationships with people in their local communities.

Twenty five years ago, people began "regionalizing" their contacts. In today's high-tech world, we can connect 24/7 around the world! We now can use Facebook, MySpace, and even Twitter to connect, build, and keep relationships top of mind.

The difficult thing with networking, socializing,

and building relationships in a home office is that it can take up the whole day. The week can slip by and no focus on work has been achieved. It is important to refer back to Chapter 3 on time management and discipline.

Social interaction should be limited. Meeting with people, especially those you want to build a strong relationship with, must be monitored and time managed.

I would recommend interacting with these people on the weekends or in the evening. The networking group should be only 1 per week. Relationships can be monitored and managed over the phone.

However, the very important professional relationships should be monitored depending on their influence with your goals. The more potential for you to achieve your goals, then the more time spent on that particular relationship.

Chapter 5 Best Practices ━━━━━━━━

1. Join one or two networking groups.
2. Monitor your time with networking and relationship building.
3. Work on networking during off-work-hour times.
4. Internet relationships are great, but face to face is still better – find a good balance between old school and new school with regards to relationship building and social interaction.

CHAPTER 6

Making It Work with Technology

What happens when your printer breaks? What happens when you fax does not go through? What happens when your high-speed Internet service goes down?

When you are working in an office environment, there is always someone within the office that can fix these issues or problems. However, when you are the only one working from home, you must become the one to fix all challenges that arise when equipment malfunctions.

The first step is to be proactive when you purchase your equipment. Make sure all equipment is purchased locally. That way if you do have issues with a printer, fax, or scanner, you can take the equipment in for repairs. Also, ask about warranties before purchasing. Buying an extended warranty or service agreement may save you money and time in the long run. Also, consult with others in your neighborhood that may also work from home. Find out which is the best Internet provider for your area.

One time while teaching a Webinar, my Internet provider system went down. I had to sprint to the closest library to conduct my conference call live meeting session. Knowing in advance where one can go in an "emergency" is a good proactive plan. Also, make sure you have all equipment backed up with your information.

Nothing is worse than losing all of your files off of your computer or laptop. Make sure your electricity has a power surge protector. Having lightning hit close by your house can destroy your equipment if you don't' take the proper action in advance.

Just like taking care of your car, make sure to service your equipment. Keep the dust out of your office. Don't leave your office with the windows open. Rain and dust can cause damage to your equipment. The best advice is to keep food and drink away from your equipment. Nothing is worse than having a beverage ruin your keyboard!

Accidents can happen, and being on guard is a good idea. Make sure others in your family are aware of your rules about your office. Having a family member talking to you while drinking a cup of coffee close to your laptop can prove to be a disaster waiting to happen. Be aware of the downfalls.

A business can be shut down for weeks by one simple spill.

Also, have a backup plan. What if the printer, fax, scanner, phone, and computer were shut down for a week? Where would you work? What would be your backup plan? Alternative areas of workspace could be the library, a hotel business center, or perhaps an Internet cafe. As long as you have a cell phone and a laptop, you can take your work on the road. Expect the best but be prepared for the worst. If you are forced to close down your home office temporarily, prepare in advance with a plan.

Best Practices for Chapter 6: ━━━━━━━

1. Buy home office equipment locally.
2. Purchase service and maintenance agreements.
3. Keep the office clean with limited food and drink around equipment.
4. Have a backup plan if your office is closed temporarily due to unplanned events.

CHAPTER 7

Final Best Practice Thoughts

Setting up a home office can be thrilling, exciting, and challenging. At times, getting started will be the hardest step. If you follow my best practice recommendations and tweak my ideas to suit your home office, you will be successful.

Remember, a home or "virtual office" was unheard of 15 years ago. Going forward into the future home/virtual offices will become the norm rather than the exception.

Due to the rising cost of transportation to and from offices and the difficult economy, many companies are being forced to push their employees into a home office environment. Also, technology has provided us the access to work from anywhere in today's world.

The changing global economy is forcing companies to think and innovate differently. How can we work and get the biggest bang for our buck type of scenario.

Working in a virtual office or home office is the key for many large companies in today's fast-changing world to cut costs.

Being informed and educated about the pitfalls of setting up a home office will be beneficial and advantageous before you begin. The process seems simple. Balancing work and life can be achieved to your advantage. Making technology work to your benefit is helpful. Being organized, disciplined, and staying motivated day in and day out is an art. With a little luck, passion, and perseverance, you will be successful. If you are like me, you will eventually become very spoiled.

Enjoy working successfully from a home office environment.

Most of all remember: "Attitude determines your Altitude."

Cecelia Jernegan
Home Office Setup Coach Specialist

LaVergne, TN USA
28 January 2011
214410LV00006B/74/P